BANKSON LANGUAGE SCREENING TEST

BANKSON LANGUAGE SCREENING TEST

by

Nicholas W. Bankson, Ph.D.

Chairman
Department of Speech Pathology
and Audiology
Boston University

University Park Press

Baltimore • London • Tokyo

UNIVERSITY PARK PRESS
International Publishers in Science and Medicine
Chamber of Commerce Building
Baltimore, Maryland 21202

Typeset by Alpha Graphics, Inc.
Manufactured in the United States of America by Bay Printing, Inc.

Library of Congress Cataloging in Publication Data
Bankson, Nicholas W.
  Bankson language screening test.

  Includes bibliographies.
  1. Bankson language screening test. I. Title.
LB1139.L3B35   372.6'044   77-5575
ISBN 0-8391-1126-6

Contents

Acknowledgments

The author wishes to express his appreciation to the following school systems and individuals for their invaluable assistance and support in the development of this test: Talbot County Public Schools, Easton, Maryland; St. Mary's County Public Schools, Leonardtown, Maryland; Fred Distler; Judy Compton; Lou Ann Bankson; Mary Blakely; Bonnie Haynes; Cheryl Pringle; Penny Donovan; and Joan Maynard.

Introduction and Test Administration

INTRODUCTION AND TEST BACKGROUND

The Bankson Language Screening Test (BLST) was developed to provide a means by which a number of psycholinguistic as well as perceptual skills could be surveyed in children in a relatively short period of time. Such a tool is particularly needed for determining those areas in need of further in-depth analysis by language tests that are diagnostic in nature. The screening instrument has sufficient breadth and depth to assist the clinician in the process of case selection and to provide a strong base from which to recommend additional testing. The BLST is an outgrowth of the author's clinical experience, which indicated that clinicians frequently rely on instruments for language screening that require a minimum of 20 minutes of administration time and yet provide data in only a single aspect of language behavior. This test is an attempt to remedy this situation through a broad based screening device that requires approximately 25 minutes for administration.

The BLST consists of a battery of 17 nine-item subtests organized into five general categories: semantic knowledge; morphological rules; syntactic rules; visual perception; and auditory perception. The test is designed to assess expressive language, and it is on this aspect of language that scoring is primarily based. Expressive language was focused on for three reasons: 1) this is the mode of language by which most observers become aware of the presence or absence of a language deficit; 2) it ultimately becomes the terminal objective in language intervention strategies; and 3) language testing materials are less readily available for expressive as opposed to receptive language.

The selection of subtests to be included in the BLST was predicated upon a review of those areas that language interventionists frequently test and remediate in younger children (McLean, Yoder, and Schiefelbusch, 1972). Historically, language assessment has focused on vocabulary development more than other aspects of language (Gesell, 1940; McCarthy, 1954). Accordingly, a semantic knowledge section of the BLST was developed that contains subtests ranging from concrete word expression (e.g., nouns, verbs) to more abstract generalizations (categories, functions, opposites). The eight semantic section subtests include the following: body parts, nouns, verbs, categories, functions, prepositions, colors/quantity, and opposites.

A second major area on which clinicians focus in language assessment and remediation is that of grammatical rules (Lee, 1974). Rules of grammar can be broken down into morphological rules and syntactic rules, and thus the second and third sections of the BLST focus on these areas. The three morphological subtests that comprise the second section of the instrument cover those areas wherein problems of this type are most likely to occur: pronoun usage, verb tense, pluralization, and use of the comparative and superlative. The two syntactic subtests cover subject-verb agreement and negation, and the child's ability to repeat sentences containing various transformations, as well as his ability to judge the grammaticality of sentences produced by the examiner.

The fourth subtest of the BLST screens visual perception. While this area is not viewed as an aspect of oral language, it was included in the screening battery for the following reasons: 1) clinicians frequently utilize visual stimuli in the remediation of receptive and expressive language problems, and thus it becomes important to ascertain whether or not gross perceptual problems may exist in this area; and 2) because children referred for oral language evaluations are often those who eventually are found to have disabilities in the area of written language, this screening allows for earlier detection of those who may need ancillary educational evaluation. Aspects of visual perception included in the two subtests include visual discrimination, association, and sequencing.

The fifth and final section of the BLST includes two auditory perception subtests covering the areas of auditory memory, sequencing, and discrimination. Language clinicians have traditionally been interested in auditory perceptual skills as they relate to language (Wiig and Semel, 1976), and thus they were included in the test.

A summary of the BLST sections and subtests is as follows:

Semantic Knowledge
Body Parts
Nouns
Verbs
Categories
Functions
Prepositions
Colors/Quantity
Opposites

Morphological Rules
Pronouns
Verb Tenses
Plurals/Comparatives/
  Superlatives

Syntactic Rules
Subject-Verb Agreement/
  Negation
Sentence Repetition/
  Judgment

Visual Perception
Matching/
  Discrimination
Association/
  Sequencing

Auditory Perception
Memory
Sequencing/
  Discrimination

Normative data on the BLST were gathered on a sample of 637 children ages 4.1 to 8.0 years. Selection of test items was based upon the kinds of linguistic and perceptual skills one would ordinarily expect children in this age range to have developed or be in the process of mastering (Bangs, 1968; Berry, 1969; Trantham

and Pedersen, 1976). Review of the percentiles established with the normative sample indicates that the instrument is more sensitive to developmental differences at the lower as opposed to the upper end of this age spectrum.

TEST ADMINISTRATION

The BLST is a relatively simple and straightforward instrument to administer, and thus intelligent and perceptive individuals can be taught in a relatively short period of time to administer and score the test. It is expected, however, that a professional person with a background in language disorders will be the person to analyze test results and make decisions related thereto. While the test is not difficult to administer, it does require familiarity with the instrument and scoring procedures to use the test reliably. There are enough differences between subtests and on occasion within subtests to warrant a minimum of five practice administrations with the instrument before using it for screening purposes. The test is designed to be administered on a one-to-one basis, with the testee seated across the table from the examiner. Testing should be done in a room that is quiet and free from distraction.

The BLST was designed to screen expressive language; however, directions are also given for administration of seven out of the eight semantic knowledge subtests on a receptive basis. This was done so that those items missed during the expressive portion of the test can be tested receptively if the examiner wishes. It is recognized that such information may be useful to the clinician. However, scoring of the test is based on only the expressive portion.

While specific directions for the administration and scoring of each of the nine-item subtests are included opposite each test plate, the following are general testing and scoring guidelines for the BLST:

1. If the examiner observes that a child did not hear and/or understand the directions, it is permissible to repeat or paraphrase the directions.

2. The examiner should have a plain sheet of paper available so that certain pictures may be covered on particular subtests.

3. The morphological rules subtests contain model or demonstration items that are necessary in order to elicit the desired responses from the testee. Therefore, it is important that one adhere to the suggested structure.

4. Items are scored as either correct or incorrect; however, the tester may wish to write descriptive comments on the score sheets. Receptive responses are considered incorrect for scoring purposes. Additional score sheets are available from the publisher.

5. In some instances more than one answer can be scored as correct. On particular items examples of appropriate alternate responses are indicated in parentheses on the score sheet. The examiner should be flexible enough to score as correct those responses that he views as plausible in light of the picture being named and/or the child's background. For example, a child might call the picture of the girl writing in Item 23, "drawing." This is a plausible response and is thus scored as correct. For Item 30, a child might say "hot dog." If the examiner has reason to believe that a particular child may eat hot dogs for breakfast, the response should be scored as correct. A method of ascertaining this is to ask what time of day you eat breakfast. For items dealing with morphological rules, substitutions for word stems can also be allowed. For example, on Item 89, "pick*ed* the flowers" may be substituted for "already climb*ed*." The examiner's judgment regarding appropriateness of response is thus allowed for.

TECHNICAL DATA

During the process of pilot work on the test its format and items were modified and refined. The present form of the BLST incorporates these revisions and supercedes its predecessor, the Talbot County Language Screening Test. The result is a comprehensive screening instrument that is self-contained in a notebook format.

The group of children on whom the test was normed consisted of 637 children between the ages of 4.1 and 8.0 years living in semi-rural counties adjacent to the Washington, D.C., metropolitan area. These youngsters were members of two preschool classes, 19 public school classes, and two parochial school classes. These classes were selected as representative of the socioeconomic levels present in this geographic area. Eighty percent of the children were White, 18 percent Black, and two percent from other nationality groups. The sample ranged from lower-middle to upper-middle socioeconomic levels, with 75 percent drawn from a strictly middle class population. All children were grouped for normative data purposes into six-month age categories beginning at 4.1 to 4.6 and progressing to 8.0 years.

RELIABILITY

Reliability of the BLST was determined in two ways. Test-retest reliability was assessed by administering the test to a group of 70 children two times, with second testing occurring one week after the original testing. Point-to-point reliability for all items was established at the .94 level. In addition to test-retest reliability, the Kuder-Richardson 20 test indicated a .96 overall reliability index.

VALIDITY

Concurrent validity of the BLST was determined by comparing the scores of 70 children on the BLST with their performances on three other widely used language tests. Pearson Produce-Moment correlations between the BLST and the other tests were as follows:

BLST and the Peabody Picture Vocabulary Test—
r = .54
BLST and the Boehm Concept Test — r = .62
BLST and the Test of Auditory Comprehension of Language — r = .64

The correlation coefficients obtained indicate that the BLST is measuring a behavioral area similar to the three comparative tests. The BLST, however, is also sampling behaviors other than those included on the other measures. It should be noted that the three comparison instruments differ from the BLST in the following ways: 1) they assess receptive as compared to expressive language, and 2) they are more circumscribed in the aspects of language upon which they focus.

Content validity of the BLST is based upon the fact that the items included in the instrument were selected as representative of the kinds of tasks that language clinicians assess and remediate. A review of pre-school and primary grade academic curricula would reflect the knowledge and skills measured in this screening instrument.

Additional correlations were obtained between selected subtests of the BLST and tests designed to measure similar language behaviors. For eighteen children a total score from the eight Semantic Knowledge subtests was correlated with their scores from the Boehm Concept Test. A resulting r value of .82 was obtained. A similar comparison was made between a total score from the five Morphological Rules, and Syntactic Rules subtests, and a child's score on a 100 utterance spontaneous language sample scored according to the Developmental Sentence Scoring criteria outlined by Lee (1974). In this instance a correlation of .76 was obtained. Both correlations were statistically significant beyond the .01 level.

These data support the validity of the BLST as a measure which screens behaviors which other instruments assess in a diagnostic fashion.

TEST INTERPRETATION

As stated earlier, the primary purpose of this instrument is to screen for children who may need language remediation, and to determine appropriate areas for further language testing. Scores obtained on the various subtests can be graphed for ease of interpretation on the language profile sheet at the end of the score sheet. Our results have indicated that children who score at the 30th percentile and below need further language assessment. Those at the 15th percentile and below are those who are most certain to be enrolled for clinical language instruction, while those from the 16th through 30th percentile are those for whom a classroom enrichment approach, directed to specific linguistic weaknesses, may be appropriate. When information regarding how a child ranks with his peers on particular subtests is desired, the examiner should refer to the table of means and standard deviations for each of the subtests.

While it is intended that a comprehensive screening of language areas will be done with the complete test battery, there may be occasions where a quick screening of language is desired. In such instances it would be appropriate to administer the 38 items from the BLST that, according to an item analysis, are most discriminating. Utilizing a minimal criterion discrimination index of .30, the following items were determined to be most discriminating: 8, 15, 31, 34, 47, 48, 49, 51, 54, 61, 62, 64, 65, 66, 67, 68, 69, 70, 71, 77, 84, 86, 87, 90, 95, 96, 97, 100, 101, 102, 104, 105, 119, 120, 121, 134, 135, 141. On the basis of performance on these items the examiner could then determine whether or not to proceed with the complete test instrument.

REFERENCES

Bangs, T. 1968. Language and Learning Disorders of the Pre-Academic Child. Appleton-Century-Crofts Inc., New York.

Berry, M. 1969. Language Disorders of Children. Appleton-Century-Crofts Inc., New York.

Gesell, A. 1940. The First Five Years of Life. Harpers, New York.

Lee, L. 1974. Developmental Sentence Analysis. Northwestern University Press, Evanston, Ill.

McCarthy, D. 1954. Language development in children. In L. Carmichael (ed.), Manual of Child Psychology, 2nd Ed. John Wiley & Sons, Inc., New York.

McLean, J., Yoder, D., and Schiefelbusch, R. 1972. Language Intervention with the Retarded. University Park Press, Baltimore.

Trantham, C., and Pedersen, J. 1976. Normal Language Development. The Williams & Wilkins Co., Baltimore.

Wiig, E., and Semel, E. 1976. Language Disabilities in Children and Adolescents. Charles E. Merrill Publishing Co., Columbus.

MEAN AND STANDARD DEVIATIONS FOR SUBTESTS

Age	Body Parts A		Nouns B		Verbs C		Categories D		Functions E		Prepositions F		Colors/ Quantity G		Opposites H	
	X	SD	X	SD	X	SD	X	SD	X	SD	X	SD	X	SD	X	SD
4.1–4.6	6.62	1.77	4.22	1.64	6.32	1.75	4.33	2.06	6.97	1.63	2.38	1.48	6.71	2.15	1.50	1.51
4.7–5.0	6.64	1.97	5.17	1.89	7.85	1.54	4.85	2.08	7.66	1.86	5.02	2.70	6.19	2.59	.85	1.63
5.1–5.6	7.25	1.73	5.99	1.93	8.33	1.36	5.74	1.74	8.00	1.58	5.76	2.73	6.60	2.46	1.96	2.49
5.7–6.0	7.48	1.29	6.34	1.64	8.67	.70	6.11	1.46	7.96	1.56	6.06	2.52	7.37	1.68	2.23	2.71
6.1–6.6	7.95	1.12	7.08	1.55	8.91	.30	6.79	.66	8.52	.74	7.08	1.96	8.05	.90	4.06	2.94
6.7–7.0	7.78	1.23	7.18	1.67	8.74	.59	6.60	1.14	8.37	.92	7.22	2.12	8.05	1.08	5.05	2.67
7.1–7.6	8.13	.87	7.71	1.28	8.71	.76	6.85	.75	8.77	.50	7.85	1.70	8.25	.89	5.71	2.03
7.7–8.0	8.31	.93	7.98	1.25	8.78	.60	6.89	.89	8.64	.77	7.62	2.02	8.11	.98	6.07	2.22

Pronouns I		Verb Tenses J		Plurals/ Comparative/ Superlative K		Subject-Verb Agreement/ Negation L		Sentence Repetition/ Judgment M		Visual Matching/ Discrimination N		Visual Association/ Sequencing O		Auditory Memory P		Auditory Sequencing/ Discrimination Q	
X	SD	X	SD	X	SD	X	SD	X	SD	X	SD	X	SD	X	SD	X	SD
4.70	2.62	5.49	2.59	3.00	1.31	5.28	2.04	5.49	1.59	3.25	1.57	4.51	1.24	7.25	1.26	6.21	1.47
6.12	2.40	5.43	2.61	3.72	1.66	6.28	2.43	5.60	2.21	3.98	1.91	5.71	2.01	5.98	2.18	6.35	1.92
6.92	1.76	6.41	2.41	4.53	1.54	6.64	2.07	6.00	1.90	4.75	2.06	6.28	1.86	6.79	1.56	6.89	1.72
6.95	1.73	6.51	2.35	4.22	1.74	6.34	2.36	6.42	1.82	5.43	2.12	6.32	2.07	6.42	2.01	6.94	1.44
7.74	1.21	7.20	1.96	5.26	1.47	7.02	2.08	6.89	1.32	6.71	1.71	7.21	1.40	7.45	1.27	7.41	1.28
7.45	1.54	6.60	2.76	5.45	2.22	6.78	2.53	7.56	1.24	6.90	1.81	7.40	1.59	7.19	1.40	7.51	1.32
7.98	1.09	7.33	2.06	5.90	1.97	7.26	2.14	7.77	.99	7.20	1.39	7.84	1.17	7.30	1.26	7.85	1.15
7.82	1.40	7.04	2.31	5.73	2.17	7.51	2.07	7.69	1.40	7.33	1.30	7.71	1.36	7.42	1.39	7.80	1.33

PERCENTILE RANKS CORRESPONDING TO RAW SCORES

Total Raw Score	Age Levels							
	n-76 4.1–4.6	n-57 4.7–5.0	n-92 5.1–5.6	n-82 5.7–6.0	n-84 6.1–6.6	n-81 6.7–7.0	n-61 7.1–7.6	n-45 7.7–8.0
147–153						100	100	100
140–146				100	100	98	98	91
133–139			100	94	96	85	77	80
126–132		100	95	91	68	64	52	51
119–125	100	96	87	79	56	43	38	31
112–118	99	89	75	68	35	36	25	27
105–111	89	79	59	55	24	26	13	16
98–104	85	65	42	40	18	22	5	9
91–97	76	46	26	26	8	15		4
84–90	62	33	18	20	2	7		4
77–83	49	25	15	13		4		
70–76	37	16	10	7		2		
63–69	29	11	4	2		2		
56–62	16	9	1	1		1		
49–55	8	5		1				
42–48	5	4						
35–41	1	2						

Bankson Language Screening Test Score Sheet

Part One: SEMANTIC KNOWLEDGE

A. *Body Parts* (Plate 1 — Items 1–9)

	E	(R)			E	(R)			E	(R)
1.	mouth	____ (____)	4.	chin	____ (____)	7.	elbow	____ (____)
2.	eye	____ (____)	5.	thumb	____ (____)	8.	ankle	____ (____)
3.	hand	____ (____)	6.	knee	____ (____)	9.	shoulder	____ (____)

B. *Nouns* (Plate 2 — Items 10–18)

	E	(R)			E	(R)			E	(R)
10.	butterfly	____ (____)	13.	lock	____ (____)	16.	doorknob	____ (____)
11.	mask	____ (____)	14.	faucet	____ (____)	17.	sofa	____ (____)
12.	umbrella	____ (____)	15.	violin	____ (____)	18.	tent	____ (____)

C. *Verbs* (Plate 3 — Items 19–27)

	E	(R)			E	(R)			E	(R)
19.	running	____ (____)	22.	swinging	____ (____)	25.	creeping (crawling)	____ (____)
20.	reading	____ (____)	23.	writing (drawing) (coloring)	____ (____)	26.	driving	____ (____)
21.	catching	____ (____)	24.	jumping	____ (____)	27.	hammering (pounding) (making something) (fixing)	____ (____)

D. *Categories* (Plate 4 — Items 28–36)

	E	(R)			E	(R)			E	(R)
28.	animals	____ (____) ____ (____)	31.	hot things	____ (____) ____ (____)	34.	tools	____ (____) ____ (____)
29.	toys	____ (____) ____ (____)	32.	furniture	____ (____) ____ (____)	35.	appliances	____ (____) ____ (____)
30.	food for breakfast	____ (____)	33.	fruits	____ (____)	36.	means of transportation	____ (____) ____ (____)

E. *Functions* (Plate 5 — Items 37–45)

	E	(R)			E	(R)			E	(R)
37.	eat with	____ (____)	40.	dig with	____ (____)	43.	tell time with	____ (____)
38.	wear	____ (____)	41.	sew with	____ (____)	44.	fix with	____ (____)
39.	write with	____ (____)	42.	ride in	____ (____)	45.	make music with	____ (____)

F. Prepositions (Plate 6 — Items 46-54)

	E	(R)			E	(R)			E	(R)
46. on	____	(____)	49. under (in front of)		____	(____)	52. around		____	(____)
47. between	____	(____)	50. behind (in back of) (through)		____	(____)	53. across (through)		____	(____)
48. under	____	(____)	51. over (above)		____	(____)	54. beside (on the side of)		____	(____)

G. Colors/Quantity (Plate 7)

Colors (Items 55-60)   *Quantity* (Items 61-63)

	E	(R)			E	(R)			E	(R)
55. red	____	(____)	58. green		____	(____)	61. more		____	(____)
56. blue	____	(____)	59. purple		____	(____)	62. most		____	(____)
57. yellow	____	(____)	60. orange		____	(____)	63. 15		____	(____)

H. Opposites (No plate utilized — Items 64-72)

	E	(R)			E	(R)			E	(R)
64. big	____	(____)	67. fat		____	(____)	70. near		____	(____)
65. tall	____	(____)	68. first		____	(____)	71. heavy		____	(____)
66. fast	____	(____)	69. easy		____	(____)	72. least		____	(____)

Part Two: MORPHOLOGICAL RULES

I. Pronouns (Plate 8 — Items 73-81)

73. This ball belongs to _____ (her).
74. This ball belongs to _____ (them; both of them).
75. And this ball belongs to _____ (him).

76. In this picture, _____ (she) is holding the ball.
77. In this picture, _____ (they) are holding the ball.
78. In this picture, _____ (he) is holding the ball.

79. This ball is _____ (hers).
80. This ball is _____ (theirs).
81. This ball is _____ (his).

J. Verb Tenses (Plate 9 — Items 82-84)

82. He likes to run. In this picture he _____ (is running).
83. She likes to read. In this picture she _____ (is reading).
84. He likes to swim. In this picture he _____ (is swimming).

(Plate 9 — Items 85-87)

85. In this picture he _____ (runs).
86. In this picture she _____ (reads).
87. In this picture he _____ (swims).

(Plate 10 — Items 88-89)

88. In this picture he is smiling, but in this picture he has already _____ (smiled).
89. In this picture the girl is climbing, but in this picture she has already _____ (climbed) (picked the flowers).

(Plate 11 — Item 90)

90. What will happen to the pan? It _____ (will fall).

K. Plurals/Comparatives/Superlatives (Plates 12, 13, 14, and 15 — Items 91–99)

91. Here is a book. Here are two _____ (books).
92. Here is a penny. Here are two _____ (pennies).
93. Here is a box. Here are two _____ (boxes).

94. Here is a child. Here are two _____ (children).
95. Here is a man. Here are two _____ (men).

96-97. This dog is not big. This dog is big. This dog is even _____ (bigger), and this dog is the _____ (biggest).

98-99. This cake is not good. This cake is good. This cake is even _____ (better), and this cake is the very _____ (best).

Part Three: SYNTACTIC RULES

L. Subject-Verb Agreement/Negation (Plates 16 and 17 — Items 100–108)

100. The cow is eating. The cows _____ (are eating).
101. The ducks are swimming. The duck _____ (is swimming).
102. They walk. She _____ (walks).
103. He walks. They _____ (walk).

104. This man is wearing a hat, but this man _____ (isn't).
105. This dog has a collar, but this dog _____ (doesn't).
106. This cake was eaten, but this cake _____ (wasn't).
107. This tree doesn't have a large trunk, but this tree _____ (does).
108. Show me who is not a boy _____ .

M. Sentence Repetition/Judgment of Correctness (No plate)

Repetition (Items 109–113)

		Correct	Incorrect
109.	The dog likes children.	____	____
110.	Mother told sister to watch the baby.	____	____
111.	Will you show your kitty to me?	____	____
112.	We have to walk because that's Billy's bike.	____	____
113.	I'll give it to you if you want it.	____	____

Judgment of Correctness (Items 114–117)

		Correct	Incorrect
114.	Me fix it.	____	____
115.	The dog running.	____	____
116.	The dish is not broken.	____	____
117.	He walk home.	____	____

Part Four: VISUAL PERCEPTION

N. Visual Matching/Discrimination

Matching (Plate 18 — Items 118–121)

	Correct	Incorrect
118.	____	____
119.	____	____
120.	____	____
121.	____	____

Discrimination (Plates 19 and 20 — Items 122–126)

	Correct	Incorrect
122.	_____	_____
123.	_____	_____
124.	_____	_____
125.	_____	_____
126.	_____	_____

O. Visual Association/Sequencing

Association (Plates 21 and 22 — Items 127–131)

	Correct	Incorrect
127.	_____	_____
128.	_____	_____
129.	_____	_____
130.	_____	_____
131.	_____	_____

Sequencing (Plates 23, 24, and 25 — Items 132–135)

	Correct	Incorrect
132.	_____	_____
133.	_____	_____
134.	_____	_____
135.	_____	_____

Part Five: AUDITORY PERCEPTION

P. Auditory Memory (No plate — Items 136–141)

		Correct	Incorrect
136.	car goat dance	_____	_____
137.	table run orange big	_____	_____
138.	feet time hit short dig	_____	_____
139.	Mary is in the car.	_____	_____
140.	I went outside to play football.	_____	_____
141.	Mama asked Sally to bring the brown dog in the house.	_____	_____

(Items 142–144)

		Correct	Incorrect
142.	Stand up and put your hands on top of your head.	_____	_____
143.	Sit down, open the book, and put it on your lap.	_____	_____
144.	Give the book to me, walk to the door, and come back to me.	_____	_____

Q. Auditory Sequencing/Discrimination

Sequencing (No plate — Items 145–147)

145.	_____
146.	_____
147.	_____

Discrimination: (Plates 26 and 27 — Items 148–153)

		Correct	Incorrect
148.	key	_____	_____
149.	soup	_____	_____
150.	rock	_____	_____

		Correct	Incorrect
151.	The coat is by the fence.	_____	_____
152.	Don't be afraid of a big mouth.	_____	_____
153.	Did you get the wash?	_____	_____

LANGUAGE PROFILE SHEET

Subtests	Number of Correct Responses									Scores
	1	2	3	4	5	6	7	8	9	
Semantic Knowledge										
A Body Parts										
B Nouns										
C Verbs										
D Categories										
E Functions										
F Prepositions										
G Colors/ Quantity										
H Opposites										
Morphological Rules										
I Pronouns										
J Verb Tenses										
K Plurals/ Comparatives/ Superlatives										
Syntactic Rules										
L Subject-Verb Agreement/ Negation										
M Sentence Repetition/ Judgment										
Visual Perception										
N Visual Matching/ Discrimination										
O Visual Association/ Sequencing										
Auditory Perception										
P Auditory Memory										
Q Auditory Sequencing/ Discrimination										

Name _____

Grade _____ Age _____

School _____

Date _____

Examiner _____

BANKSON LANGUAGE SCREENING TEST

Plate 1

Part One: SEMANTIC KNOWLEDGE

A. Body Parts (Plate 1 — Items 1–9)

Expressive:
"Here is a picture of a boy. I want you to name the part of him that I point to."
Receptive:
"Now I want you to point to the part of him that I name."

		E	(R)			E	(R)			E	(R)
1.	mouth	____	(____)	4.	chin	____	(____)	7.	elbow	____	(____)
2.	eye	____	(____)	5.	thumb	____	(____)	8.	ankle	____	(____)
3.	hand	____	(____)	6.	knee	____	(____)	9.	shoulder	____	(____)

Plate 2

B. Nouns (Plate 2 — Items 10–18)

Expressive:
   "I am going to show you some pictures and I want you to name them for me."
Receptive:
   "Now I want you to point to the pictures that I name."

		E	(R)			E	(R)			E	(R)
10.	butterfly	____	(____)	13.	lock	____	(____)	16.	doorknob	____	(____)
11.	mask	____	(____)	14.	faucet	____	(____)	17.	sofa	____	(____)
12.	umbrella	____	(____)	15.	violin	____	(____)	18.	tent	____	(____)

Plate 3

C. *Verbs* (Plate 3 — Items 19–27)

Expressive:
"Tell me what the child is doing."
Receptive:
"Now I would like you to point to the picture in which the child is _____."

		E	(R)				E	(R)				E	(R)
19.	running	___	(___)	22.	swinging		___	(___)	25.	creeping (crawling)		___	(___)
20.	reading	___	(___)	23.	writing (drawing) (coloring)		___	(___)	26.	driving		___	(___)
21.	catching	___	(___)	24.	jumping		___	(___)	27.	hammering (pounding) (making something) (fixing)		___	(___)

Plate 4

125272

D. Categories (Plate 4 — Items 28–36)

Expressive:
   Cover the plate and say "I would like you to name some things for me.
   Name me some _____ ."
Receptive:
   "Now I want you to look at these pictures and point to the ones that I name."

		E	(R)			E	(R)			E	(R)
28.	animals	___	(___)	31.	hot things	___	(___)	34.	tools	___	(___)
		___	(___)			___	(___)			___	(___)
29.	toys	___	(___)	32.	furniture	___	(___)	35.	appliances	___	(___)
		___	(___)			___	(___)			___	(___)
30.	food for breakfast	___	(___)	33.	fruits	___	(___)	36.	means of transportation	___	(___)
		___	(___)			___	(___)			___	(___)

Plate 5

E. Functions (Plate 5 — Items 37–45)

Expressive:
Cover the plate and say "I am going to ask you to name some things for me.
Name me something we _____ ."
Receptive:
Uncover plate and say "Now I would like you to point to the pictures that I ask for.
Point to something we _____ ."

		E	(R)			E	(R)			E	(R)
37.	eat with	____	(____)	40.	dig with	____	(____)	43.	tell time with	____	(____)
38.	wear	____	(____)	41.	sew with	____	(____)	44.	fix with	____	(____)
39.	write with	____	(____)	42.	ride in	____	(____)	45.	make music with	____	(____)

Plate 6

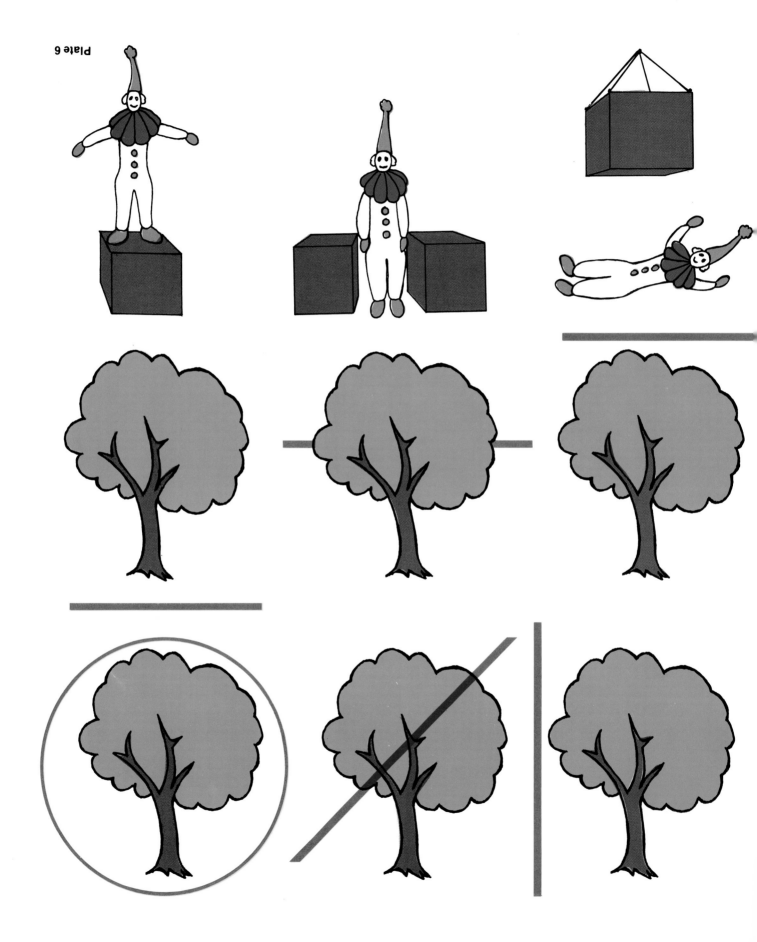

F. Prepositions (Plate 6 — Items 46–54)

Expressive:
Point to the first picture and say "Can you *tell* me where the clown is?"
If the child does not respond appropriately, expand the directions to: "See the box?
See the clown? Where is the clown?" For items 49–54 say "Tell me where the line is."
Receptive:
"This time I want you to point to the picture that I name. The clown is _____ the box."
Or, "The line is _____ the tree."

		E	(R)			E	(R)			E	(R)
46.	on	___	(___)	49.	under (in front of)	___	(___)	52.	around	___	(___)
47.	between	___	(___)	50.	behind (in back of) (through)	___	(___)	53.	across (through)	___	(___)
48.	under	___	(___)	51.	over (above)	___	(___)	54.	beside (on the side of)	___	(___)

Plate 7

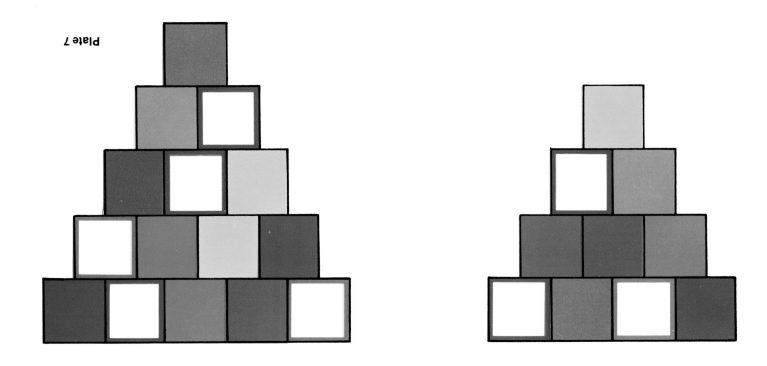

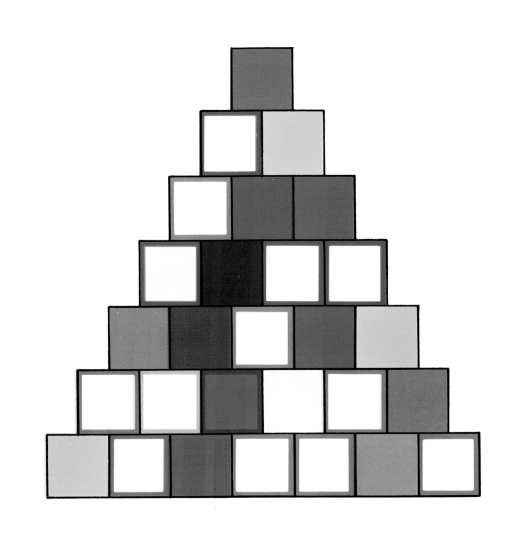

G. *Colors/Quantity* (Plate 7)

Colors (Items 55–60)

Expressive:
"Here are some different colors for you to look at. Let's see if you can name them for me."
Receptive:
"Let's see if you can point to the colors I name."

	E	(R)			E	(R)
55. red	_____	(_____)	58.	green	_____	(_____)
56. blue	_____	(_____)	59.	purple	_____	(_____)
57. yellow	_____	(_____)	60.	orange	_____	(_____)

Quantity (Items 61–63)

Expressive:
Items 61 and 62 are presented in succession so that continuity is maintained. Directions for each
item are as follows. Item 61: Expressive — The examiner points to the picture in the upper
right corner and then shifts to the pile on the upper left saying "This pile has a lot of blocks, but
this pile has even _____ (more)." Item 62: Expressive — "This pile has the _____ (most)."
Item 63: Point to pile of blocks in upper left and say "Count the blocks." Score as correct if child counts to 15.
Receptive:
Item 61: "Which pile has more?"
Item 62: "Which pile has the most?"

	E	(R)
61. more	_____	(_____)
62. most	_____	(_____)
63. 15	_____	(_____)

H. *Opposites* (No plate utilized — Items 64–72)

Expressive only:
"I am going to name a word, and I want you to tell me a word that means just the opposite."
Examiner will *gesture* as he reads the following example to the child: "The opposite
of up is down." Use other examples if necessary.

64. big	_____	67. fat	_____	70. near	_____
65. tall	_____	68. first	_____	71. heavy	_____
66. fast	_____	69. easy	_____	72. least	_____

Plate 8

Part Two: MORPHOLOGICAL RULES

I. *Pronouns*   (Plate 8 — Items 73–81)

Directions:
"Now I want us to take a look at some pictures and we'll say some things together.
I'll say part of a sentence, and then you will say part. Let's look at the first picture.
In this picture:"
Model:
"This ball belongs to him." (Object Pronoun)

73.   This ball belongs to _____ (her).
74.   This ball belongs to _____ (them; both of them).
75.   And this ball belongs to _____ (him).

Model:
"In this picture he is holding the ball." (Subject Pronoun)

76.   In this picture, _____ (she) is holding the ball.
77.   In this picture, _____ (they) are holding the ball.
78.   In this picture, _____ (he) is holding the ball.

Model:
"This ball is his." (Possessive Pronoun)

79.   This ball is _____ (hers).
80.   This ball is _____ (theirs).
81.   This ball is _____ (his).

Plate 9

J. Verb Tenses

Directions:
"I am going to say some sentences for you, and then I want you to finish part of some sentences that I start."

(Plate 9 — Items 82-84)
Model:
"He likes to swim. In this picture he is swimming." (Present Progressive)

82. He likes to run. In this picture he _____ (is running).
83. She likes to read. In this picture she _____ (is reading).
84. He likes to swim. In this picture he _____ (is swimming).

(Plate 9 — Items 85-87)

Model:
"In this picture he swims." (Present Tense).

85. In this picture he _____ (runs).
86. In this picture she _____ (reads).
87. In this picture he _____ (swims).

Plate 10

Verb Tenses - continued

(Plate 10 — Items 88–89)

Model:
"In this picture the duck is quacking, but in this picture the duck has already quacked." (Past Tense)

88. In this picture he is smiling, but in this picture he has already _____ (smiled).
89. In this picture the girl is climbing, but in this picture she has already _____ (climbed) (picked the flowers).

Plate 11

Verb Tenses - continued

(Plate 11 — Item 90)

No model required (Future Tense)

90. What will happen to the pan? It _____ (will fall).

Plate 12

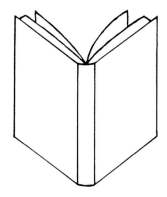

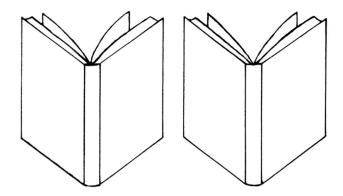

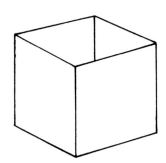

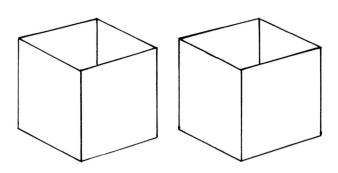

K. Plurals/Comparatives/Superlatives (Plates 12, 13, 14, and 15 — Items 91-99)

Directions:

"Again I am going to say part of a sentence, and I want you to say the rest."

91. Here is a book. Here are two _____ (books).
92. Here is a penny. Here are two _____ (pennies).
93. Here is a box. Here are two _____ (boxes).

Plate 13

Plurals - continued

94. Here is a child. Here are two _____ (children).
95. Here is a man. Here are two _____ (men).

Plate 14

Comparatives/Superlatives

96–97.   This dog is not big. This dog is big. This dog is even _____ (bigger), and this dog is the _____ (biggest).

Plate 15

Comparatives/Superlatives - continued

98-99.   This cake is not good. This cake is good. This cake is even _____ (better), and this cake is the very
_____ (best).

Plate 16

Part Three: SYNTACTIC RULES

L. Subject-Verb Agreement/Negation (Plates 16 and 17 — Items 100-108)

Directions:
"I will say part of a sentence and I want you to say the rest."

100. The cow is eating. The cows _____ (are eating).
101. The ducks are swimming. The duck _____ (is swimming).
102. They walk. She _____ (walks).
103. He walks. They _____ (walk).

Plate 17

Negation

104. This man is wearing a hat, but this man ⎯⎯⎯⎯⎯⎯ (isn't).
105. This dog has a collar, but this dog ⎯⎯⎯⎯⎯⎯ (doesn't).
106. This cake was eaten, but this cake ⎯⎯⎯⎯⎯⎯ (wasn't).
107. This tree doesn't have a large trunk, but this tree ⎯⎯⎯⎯⎯⎯ (does).
108. Show me who is not a boy ⎯⎯⎯⎯⎯⎯ .

M. Sentence Repetition/Judgment of Correctness (No plate)

Repetition   (Items 109–113)

Directions:
"I am going to say a sentence. When I am finished I want you to say exactly what I said. First it is my turn and then it will be your turn." A sentence must be identical to the model to be scored as correct.

		Correct	Incorrect
109.	The dog likes children.	_____	_____
110.	Mother told sister to watch the baby.	_____	_____
111.	Will you show your kitty to me?	_____	_____
112.	We have to walk because that's Billy's bike.	_____	_____
113.	I'll give it to you if you want it.	_____	_____

Judgment of Correctness   (Items 114–117)

Directions:
"Now I want you to be the teacher and tell me if I say it right."

		Correct	Incorrect
114.	Me fix it.	_____	_____
115.	The dog running.	_____	_____
116.	The dish is not broken.	_____	_____
117.	He walk home.	_____	_____

Plate 18

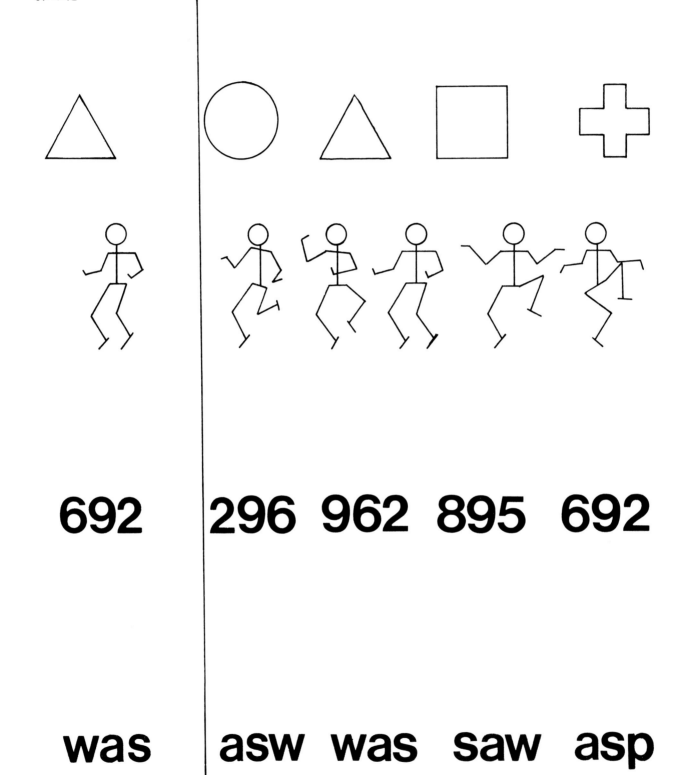

692 | 296 962 895 692

was | asw was saw asp

Part Four: VISUAL PERCEPTION

N. Visual Matching/Discrimination

Matching   (Plate 18 — Items 118–121)
Directions:
"Find the picture that matches the one I point to."

	Correct	Incorrect
118.	_____	_____
119.	_____	_____
120.	_____	_____
121.	_____	_____

Plate 19

Discrimination   (Plates 19 and 20 — Items 122–126)

Directions:
"Choose the picture that doesn't belong."

	Correct	Incorrect
122.	_____	_____
123.	_____	_____
124.	_____	_____

Plate 20

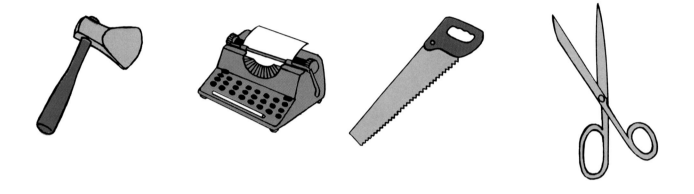

Discrimination - continued

	Correct	Incorrect
125.	_____	_____
126.	_____	_____

Plate 21

O. Visual Association/Sequencing

Association   (Plates 21 and 22 — Items 127–131)

Directions:
"Show me a picture that goes with the one I point to."

	Correct	Incorrect
127.	_____	_____
128.	_____	_____
129.	_____	_____

Plate 22

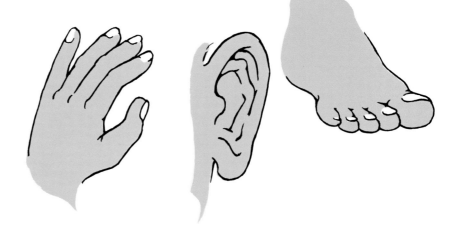

Visual Association - continued

	Correct	Incorrect
130.		
131.		

Plate 23

Sequencing   (Plates 23, 24, and 25 — Items 132–135)

Directions:
Examiner exposes only top row of stimuli for each test item, and says: "I am going to show you some pictures that are lined up." Pointing to each consecutive picture the examiner says: "This one here, this one here, etc. Look at them carefully because after you've looked for a minute I am going to see if you can remember how they were lined up." Allow child five seconds to observe stimuli. Then move cover from bottom item up to cover the initial stimulus items.

	Correct	Incorrect
132.	_____	_____

Plate 24

Visual Sequencing - continued

	Correct	Incorrect
133.	_____	_____

Plate 25

A	C	A
C	A	A
A	C	A

4	8	9	3
8	9	4	3
4	8	9	3
3	9	8	4

Visual Sequencing - continued

	Correct	Incorrect
134.	_____	_____
135.	_____	_____

Plate 26